Become One With The Universe
Through Meditation

SHADING THE POWER
OF THE MANDALA

by Authors
Lyn Ragan and Dorothy Pigue

Cover and Book Design by *Lyn M Oney*
Illustrations © Lyn Ragan and Dorothy Pigue
Trade paper ISBN 978-0-9860205-6-8

Any Internet references contained in the work are current at publication time, but the authors cannot guarantee that a specific location will continue to be maintained.

To our Dear Ones in Heaven,
With Love and Grace…

Other Books by Lyn Ragan & Dorothy Pigue

Shading The Colors of Grief and Healing
An Adult Coloring Book To Help Heal Through Grief
fb/shadingthecolorsoflife

Coloring The Shades of Grief and Healing
A Teen/Young Adult Coloring Book To Help Heal Through Grief
fb/shadingthecolorsoflife

Shading Spiritual Signs & Symbols
An Adult Coloring Book
fb/shadingthecolorsoflife

Other Books by Lyn Ragan

Wake Me Up! a true story
How Chip's Afterlife Saved Me
fb/wakemeupbook

We Need To Talk
Living With The Afterlife
fb/weneedtotalkbook

Signs From The Afterlife
Identifying Gifts From The Other Side
fb/signsfromtheafterlife

Signs From Pets In The Afterlife
Identifying Messages From Pets In Heaven
fb/signsfrompetsintheafterlife

Introduction

Lyn Ragan lost the *love of her life* in 2008. One second they were chatting on the phone and in the next, he was killed while preparing for work.

Her grief spiraled into a web of sadness she found difficult to break free of. All of their future dreams destroyed and her life altered forever, Lyn was taken by surprise when she started receiving communications from her deceased fiancé— via dreams. Ms. Ragan would later write about their visits and eventually publish several books on the subject of *Afterlife Communications*.

Her mission in life is to help those who grieve from the loss of a loved one; her ultimate goal to replace painful grief with belief and understanding. Lyn works tirelessly helping those she can reach to understand this physical life is not the end of who we are, and that love and life lives forever— as do our Souls.

Dorothy Pigue was born into a family of clairvoyants. As a young child, she began hearing the voices of spirits around her. It took many years for Dorothy to realize she could communicate with the spirit world and with loved ones who have crossed over. Wanting to enhance her gifts and psychic abilities, she trained with Carl Woodall at the *Atlanta Metaphysical Center* in Atlanta, Georgia, and became a graduate of *The Anastasi System of Psychic Development* in 2014.

Dorothy is also a Master Herbalist who has been practicing as a Korean Medicine Woman since 1996. She is a Clinical Certified Hypnotherapist, a Certified Usui/Holy Fire Reiki ® Practitioner, and an author.

Dorothy's mission in life is to share her gifts and abilities in hopes of removing the *pain of grief*. Healing begins with love and from the other side, *Love* is the message she enjoys sharing.

Authors Lyn Ragan and Dorothy Pigue are excited to come together on a personal undertaking to help bring peace, love, and healing into the hearts of those who grieve.

Becoming One With The Universe...

*A*ttention is the glue that holds our lives together. What we attend to, steers our behavior and directs our happiness. Your happiness— is determined by how you allocate your attention.

Through Meditation, we are able to adapt a more peaceful mind, improve memory, and become more productive in life. In time, meditation reduces ill-tempered impressions, anxious energies, and helps us to be more understanding and loving toward others.

Meditation doesn't have to be intensive to be effective. Five minutes each day, sitting quietly and limiting the left-brain's noisy thoughts, assists us in centering ourselves and becoming much more attentive.

" *Meditation Equals Happy Self* "

By doing something as simple as coloring, studying, or gazing at the complexity each illustration this coloring book, *Shading The Power Of The Mandala*, carries, you are effectively training your brain to be less active and teaching it to properly focus.

In essence, you are MEDITATING...

Become One With The Universe

Meditation brings wisdom;
lack of mediation leaves ignorance.
Know well what leads you forward
and what holds you back,
and choose the path that leads
to wisdom.
~Buddha

Become One With The Universe

There are two mistakes
one can make
along the road to truth:
not going all the way,
and not starting.
~Buddha

Become One With The Universe

What we are today
comes from our thoughts
of yesterday,
and our present thoughts
build our life of tomorrow.
Our life is the creation of our mind.
~Buddha

Become One With The Universe

If you have time to breathe,
you have time to meditate.
You breathe when you walk.
You breathe when you stand.
You breathe when you lie down.
~Ajahn Amaro

Become One With The Universe

*Meditation practice isn't about
trying to throw ourselves away
and become something better;
it's about befriending
who we are.*
~Ani Pema Chodron

Become One With The Universe

If every 8-year old in the world
is taught meditation,
we will eliminate violence
from the world
within one generation.
~Dalai Lama

Become One With The Universe

Don't worry about whether
you are making progress
or not.
Just keep your attention on
the Self
twenty-four hours a day.
Meditation is not something
that should be done
in a particular position
at a particular time.
It is an awareness
and an attitude
that must persist
through the day.
~Annamalai Swami

Become One With The Universe

If one thinks of oneself as free,
one is free,
and if one thinks of oneself as bound,
one is bound.
Here this saying is true,
"As one thinks, so one becomes."
~Ashtavakra Gita

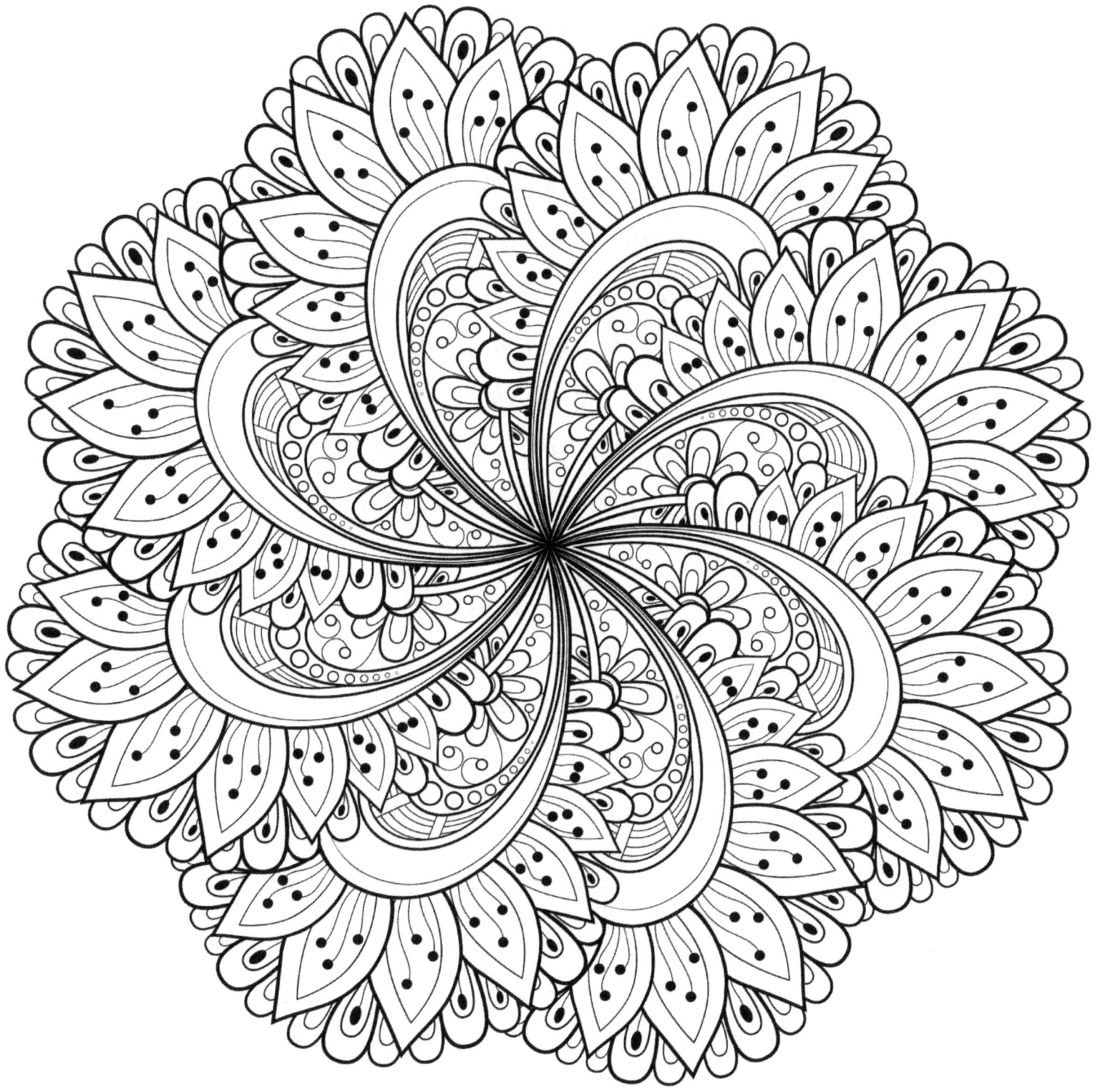

Become One With The Universe

Be still

and know yourself as the Truth

you have been searching for.

Be still

and let the inherent joy of that Truth

capture your drama

and destroy it in the bliss

of consummation.

Be still

and let your life be lived

by the purpose you were made for.

Be still

and receive the inherent truth

of your heart.

~Gangaji

Become One With The Universe

Touch your inner space,

which is nothingness,

as silent and empty as the sky;

it is your inner sky.

Once you settle down in your inner sky,

you have come home,

and a great maturity arises

in your actions,

in your behavior.

Then whatever you do has grace in it.

Then whatever you do

is a poetry in itself.

You live poetry;

your walking becomes dancing,

your silence becomes music.

~Osho

Become One With The Universe

Meditation is a process

of lightening up,

of trusting the basic goodness

of what we have and who we are,

and of realizing that any wisdom that exists,

exists in what we already have.

We can lead our life

so as to become more awake

to who we are

and what we're doing

rather than trying to improve

or change

or get rid of

who we are

or what we're doing.

The key is to wake up,

to become more alert,

more inquisitive

and curious about ourselves.

~Pema Chodron

Become One With The Universe

When your attention moves

into the Now,

there is an alertness.

It is as if you were waking up

from a dream,

the dream of thought,

the dream of past

and future.

Such clarity,

such simplicity.

No room for problem-making.

Just this moment as it is.

~Eckhart Tolle

Become One With The Universe

Meditation will not carry you
to another world,
but it will reveal the most profound
and awesome dimensions
of the world in which you already live.
Calmly contemplating these dimensions
and bringing them into the service
of compassion and kindness
is the right way
to make rapid gains
in meditation
as well as in life.
~Zen Master Hsing Yun

Become One With The Universe

All that is necessary
to awaken to yourself
as the radiant emptiness of spirit
is to stop seeking something more
or better
or different,
and to turn your attention
inward to the awake silence
that you are.
~Adyashanti

Become One With The Universe

Clarity is part of the mind
from the beginning,
a natural awareness.
Just acknowledge it,
simply notice that you're aware.
At any given moment,
you can choose to follow
the chain of thoughts,
emotions,
and sensations
that reinforce a perception
of yourself as vulnerable
and limited
or to remember
that your true nature is pure,
unconditioned,
and incapable of being harmed.
~Mingyur Rinpoche

Become One With The Universe

Meditation is meeting eternity
in the present moment.
It is resolving every problem
as it comes.
It is resolving every tension
as it creeps in.
It is facing the challenges of life
in a non-fearful way.
~Vimala Thakar

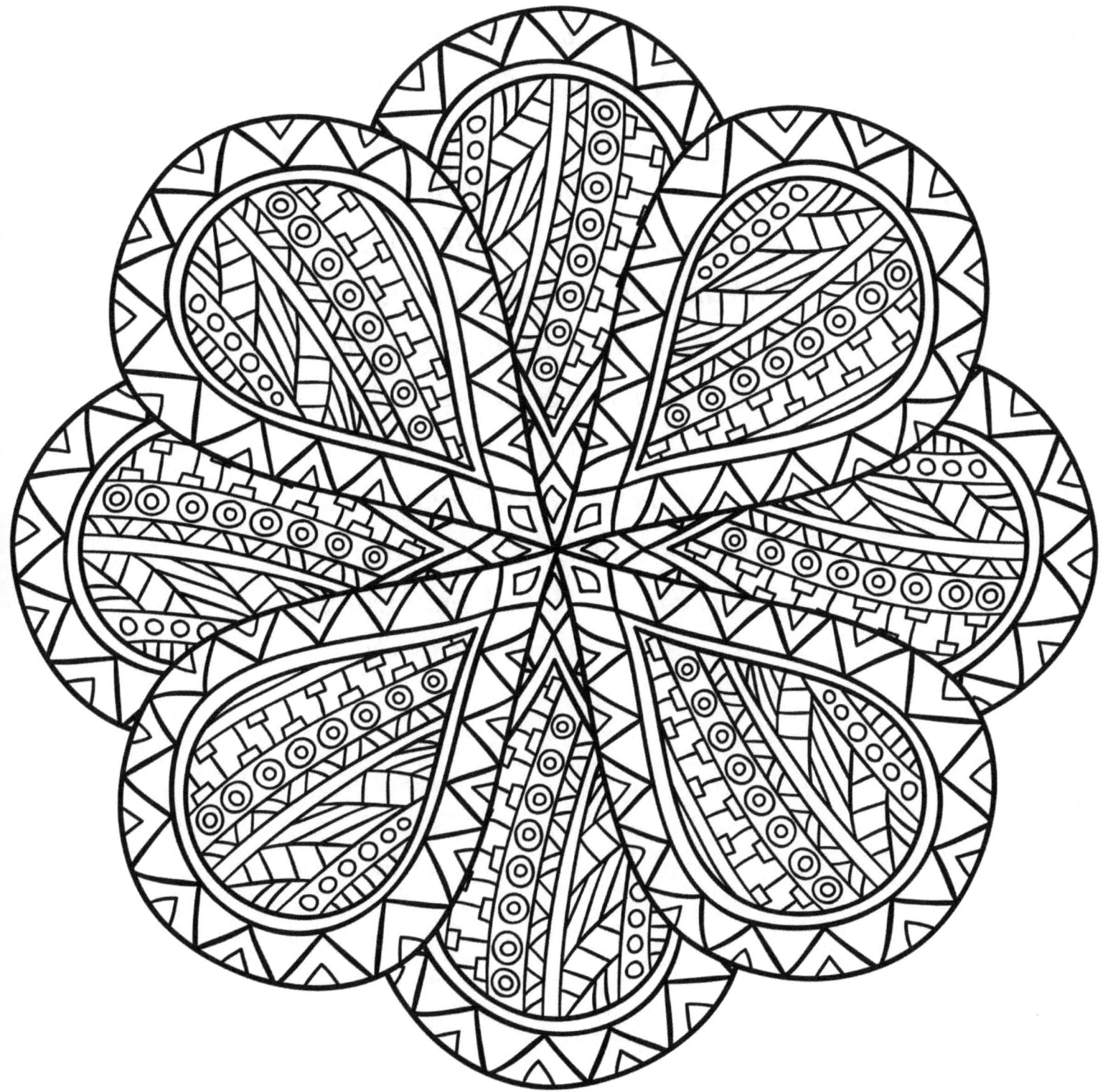

Become One With The Universe

Meditation should not be regarded
as a learning process.
It should be regarded
as an experiencing process.
You should not try to learn
from meditation but try to feel it.
Meditation is an act of nonduality.
The technique you are using
should not be separate from you;
it is you,
you are the technique.
Meditator and meditation are one.
There is no relationship involved.
~Chogyam Trungpa Rinpoche

Become One With The Universe

When we raise ourselves through meditation

to what unites us with the spirit,

we quicken something within us

that is eternal

and unlimited

by birth

and death.

Once we have experienced

this eternal part in us,

we can no longer doubt

its existence.

Meditation is thus the way to knowing

and beholding the eternal,

indestructible,

essential centre of our being.

~Rudolf Steiner

Become One With The Universe

Mindfulness helps us get better
at seeing the difference between
what's happening
and the stories
we tell ourselves about what's happening,
stories that get in the way
of direct experience.
Often such stories
treat a fleeting state of mind
as if it were our entire
and permanent self.
~Sharon Salzberg

Become One With The Universe

When you have achieved
a state of deep meditation,
you unlock the door
to your subconscious mind.
That is where the power
to create the life
you desire lies.
~Adrian Calabrese

Become One With The Universe

I said to my soul,

be still and wait

without hope,

for hope would be hope

for the wrong thing;

wait without love,

for love would be love

of the wrong thing;

there is yet faith,

but the faith and the love

are all in the waiting.

Wait without thought,

for you are not ready

for thought:

So the darkness shall be

the light,

and the stillness

the dancing.

~T.S. Eliot

Become One With The Universe

Through my love for you,
I want to express my love
for the whole cosmos,
the whole of humanity,
and all beings.
By living with you,
I want to learn to love
everyone and all species.
If I succeed in loving you,
I will be able to love everyone
and all species on Earth...
This is the real message of love.

~Thich Nhat Hanh, Teaching on Love

Become One With The Universe

It does not matter
how long you are spending
on the earth,
how much money you have gathered
or how much attention
you have received.
It is the amount of positive vibration
you have radiated in life
that matters.

~Amit Ray, Meditaiton: Insights and Inspirations

Become One With The Universe

The mind can go
in a thousand directions,
but on this beautiful path,
I walk in peace.
With each step,
the wind blows.
With each step,
a flower blooms.
~Thich Nhat Hanh

Become One With The Universe

Om is not just a sound
or vibration.
It is not just a symbol.
It is the entire cosmos,
whatever we can see,
touch, hear and feel.
Moreover, it is all that is within
our perception and all that is beyond
our perception.
It is the core of our very existence.
If you think of Om only as a sound,
a technique or a symbol of the Divine,
you will miss it altogether.
Om is the mysterious cosmic energy
that is the substratum of all the things
and all the beings of the entire universe.
It is an eternal song of the Divine.
It is continuously resounding in silence
on the background of everything
that exists.
~Amit Ray, Om Chanting and Meditation

Become One With The Universe

Meditation is the dissolution
of thoughts in Eternal awareness
or Pure consciousness
without objectification,
knowing without thinking,
merging finitude
in infinity.
~Voltaire

Become One With The Universe

The man who fears to be alone
will never be anything but lonely,
no matter how much
he may surround himself with people.
But the man who learns,
in solitude and recollection,
to be at peace with his own loneliness,
and to prefer its reality to the illusion
of merely natural companionship,
comes to know
the invisible companionship
of God.
Such a one is alone with God
in all places,
and he alone truly enjoys
the companionship of other men,
because he loves them
in God
in Whom
their presence is not tiresome,
and because of Whom
his own love for them can never know satiety.
~Thomas Merton, No Man Is an Island

Become One With The Universe

If you just sit and observe,
you will see how restless your mind is.
If you try to calm it,
it only makes it worse,
but over time it does calm,
and when it does,
there's room to hear more subtle things
- that's when your intuition starts to blossom
and you start to see things more clearly
and be in the present more.
Your mind just slows down,
and you see a tremendous expanse
in the moment.
You see so much more
than you could see before.
It's a discipline;
you have to practice it.
~Walter Isaacson, Steve Jobs

Become One With The Universe

It is never too late to turn on the light.

Your ability to break an unhealthy habit

or turn off an old tape

doesn't depend on how long it has been running;

a shift in perspective doesn't depend

on how long you've held on to the old view.

When you flip the switch in that attic,

it doesn't matter whether its been dark

for ten minutes,

ten years

or ten decades.

The light still illuminates the room

and banishes the murkiness,

letting you see the things

you couldn't see before.

Its never too late

to take a moment to look.

~Sharon Salzberg, Real Happiness: The Power of Meditation

Become One With The Universe

If everything happens
for a reason
that means you made
the right choice
even when it's
the wrong choice.
~Treyco

Become One With The Universe

It is only through meditation
that we can get lasting peace,
divine peace.
If we meditate soulfully in the morning
and receive peace for only one minute,
that one minute of peace
will permeate our whole day.
And when we have a meditation
of the highest order,
then we really get abiding peace,
light and delight.
We need meditation
because we want to grow in light
and fulfill ourselves in light.
If this is our aspiration,
if this is our thirst,
then meditation
is the only way.

~Sri Chinmoy, The Wisdom of Sri Chinmoy

Become One With The Universe

Meditation practice is like piano scales,
basketball drills, ballroom dance class.
Practice requires discipline;
it can be tedious; it is necessary.
After you have practiced enough,
you become more skilled
at the art form itself.
You do not practice to become a great scale player
or drill champion.
You practice to become a musician
or athlete.
Likewise, one does not practice meditation
to become a great meditator.
We meditate to wake up and live,
to become skilled
at the art of living.

~Elizabeth Lesser, The Seeker's Guide:
Making Your Life a Spiritual Adventure